Mel Bay Presents

Solo Pieces for the BEGINNING TREBLE/ALTO RECORDER

By Costel Puscoiu

1 2 3 4 5 6 7 8 9 0

© 2001 BY MEL BAY PUBLICATIONS, INC., PACIFIC, MO 63069.
ALL RIGHTS RESERVED. INTERNATIONAL COPYRIGHT SECURED. B.M.I. MADE AND PRINTED IN U.S.A.
No part of this publication may be reproduced in whole or in part, or stored in a retrieval system, or transmitted in any form
or by any means, electronic, mechanical, photocopy, recording, or otherwise, without written permission of the publisher.

Visit us on the Web at www.melbay.com — E-mail us at email@melbay.com

Contents

		Piano	Alto Recorder
Spring	Costel Puscoiu	3	3
Madrigal	Michael Praetorius	4	3
Hungarian Dance (No.1)	Johannes Brahms	5	3
Air (from Sonata No.9)	Wolfgang Amadeus Mozart	6	4
Easy	Costel Puscoiu	8	4
March	Costel Puscoiu	9	6
Greensleeves	Old English Song	10	6
Gavotte	Arcangelo Corelli	12	7
Melody	Costel Puscoiu	13	7
Papageno's Carillon	Wolfgang Amadeus Mozart	14	7
Tiribomba	Italian Folk Song	15	9
The Beginner	Costel Puscoiu	16	9
Melody	Nicolai Rimsky-Korsakov	17	9
Moscow Nights	Russian Folk Song	18	10
Children's Dance	Costel Puscoiu	19	10
Krakowiak	Polish Folk Song	20	10
Pavane	Gabriel Fauré	21	11
Adagio (from Clarinet Concerto)	Wolfgang Amadeus Mozart	22	11
Prelude (Op.28, No.7)	Frédéric Chopin	24	13
Two Pigeons	Argentinian Folk Song	25	13
Morning (from "Peer Gynt")	Edvard Grieg	26	13
Album – leaf (from "Lyric Pieces")	Edvard Grieg	28	14
Slavonic Dance (Op.46, No.2)	Antonin Dvořák	30	15
Romance (Op.50)	Ludwig van Beethoven	31	15

Spring

Costel Puscoiu
(1951)

Madrigal

Michael Praetorius
(1571 - 1621)

Hungarian Dance
(No. 1)

Johannes Brahms
(1833 - 1897)

Air
(from Sonata No. 9)

Wolfgang Amadeus Mozart
(1756 - 1791)

Easy

Costel Puscoiu
(1951)

March

Costel Puscoiu
(1951)

Greensleeves

Old English Song

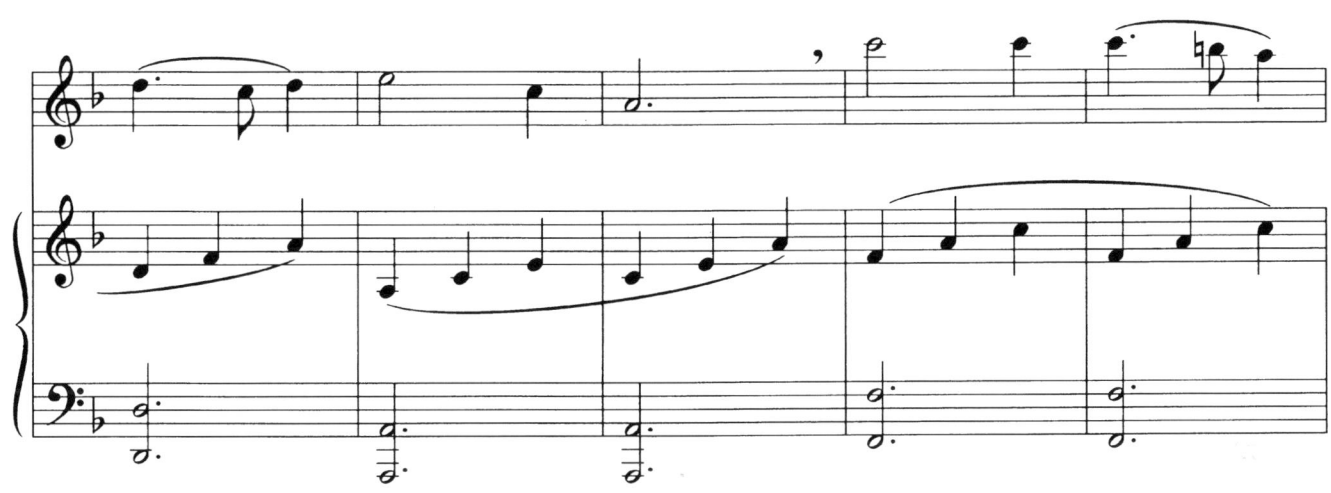

Gavotte

Arcangelo Corelli
(1653 - 1713)

Melody

Costel Puscoiu
(1951)

Papageno's Carillon
(from "The Magic Flute")

Wolfgang Amadeus Mozart
(1756 - 1791)

Tiribomba

Italian Folk Song

The Beginner

Costel Puscoiu
(1951)

Mel Bay Presents
Solo Pieces
for the
BEGINNING TREBLE/ALTO RECORDER

By Costel Puscoiu

Treble/Alto Recorder

© 2001 BY MEL BAY PUBLICATIONS, INC., PACIFIC, MO 63069.
ALL RIGHTS RESERVED. INTERNATIONAL COPYRIGHT SECURED. B.M.I. MADE AND PRINTED IN U.S.A.
No part of this publication may be reproduced in whole or in part, or stored in a retrieval system, or transmitted in any form
or by any means, electronic, mechanical, photocopy, recording, or otherwise, without written permission of the publisher.

Visit us on the Web at www.melbay.com — E-mail us at email@melbay.com

Contents

		Piano	Alto Recorder
Spring	Costel Puscoiu	3	3
Madrigal	Michael Praetorius	4	3
Hungarian Dance (No.1)	Johannes Brahms	5	3
Air (from Sonata No.9)	Wolfgang Amadeus Mozart	6	4
Easy	Costel Puscoiu	8	4
March	Costel Puscoiu	9	6
Greensleeves	Old English Song	10	6
Gavotte	Arcangelo Corelli	12	7
Melody	Costel Puscoiu	13	7
Papageno's Carillon	Wolfgang Amadeus Mozart	14	7
Tiribomba	Italian Folk Song	15	9
The Beginner	Costel Puscoiu	16	9
Melody	Nicolai Rimsky-Korsakov	17	9
Moscow Nights	Russian Folk Song	18	10
Children's Dance	Costel Puscoiu	19	10
Krakowiak	Polish Folk Song	20	10
Pavane	Gabriel Fauré	21	11
Adagio (from Clarinet Concerto)	Wolfgang Amadeus Mozart	22	11
Prelude (Op.28, No.7)	Frédéric Chopin	24	13
Two Pigeons	Argentinian Folk Song	25	13
Morning (from "Peer Gynt")	Edvard Grieg	26	13
Album – leaf (from "Lyric Pieces")	Edvard Grieg	28	14
Slavonic Dance (Op.46, No.2)	Antonin Dvořák	30	15
Romance (Op.50)	Ludwig van Beethoven	31	15

Spring

Costel Puscoiu
(1951)

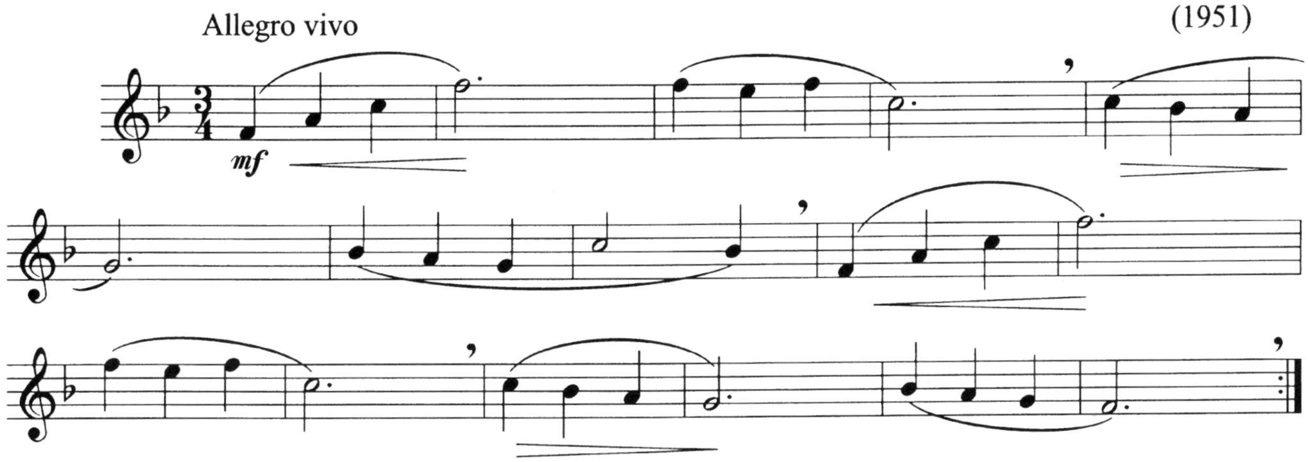
Allegro vivo
mf

Madrigal

Michael Praetorius
(1571 - 1621)

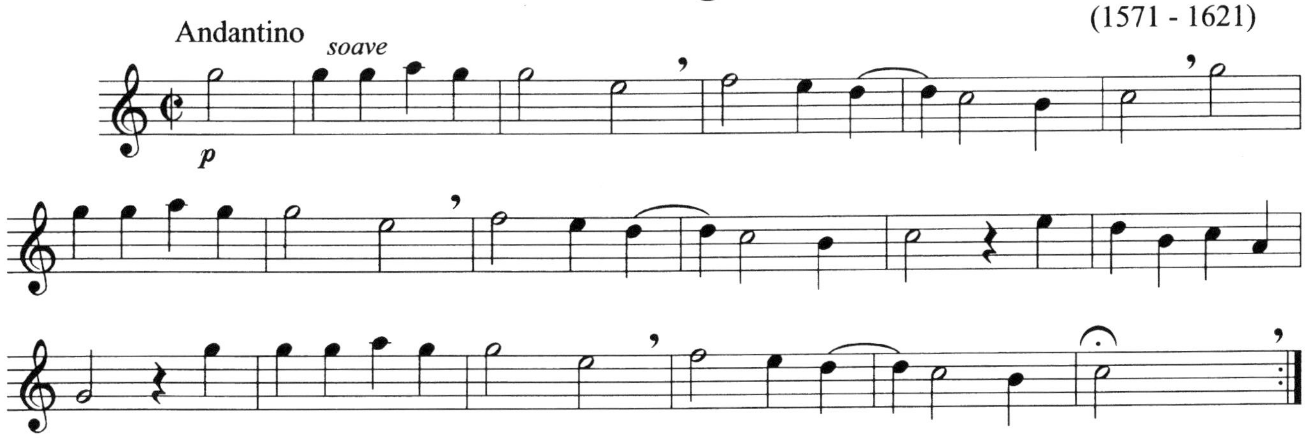
Andantino
soave
p

Hungarian Dance

(No.1)

Johannes Brahms
(1833 - 1897)

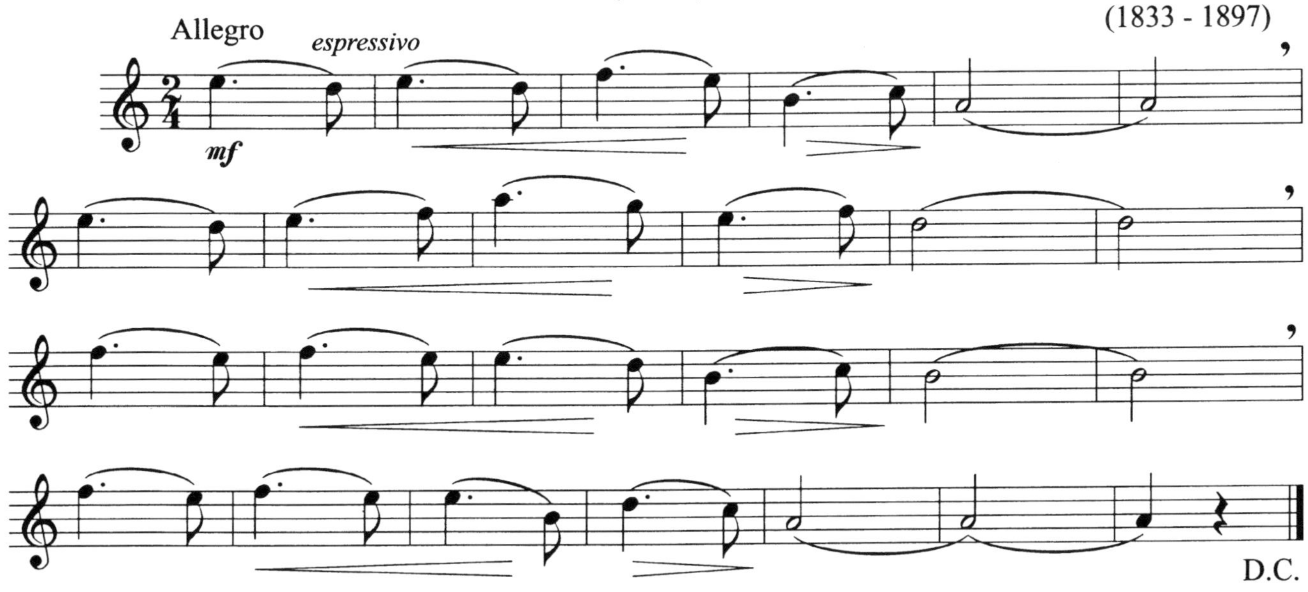
Allegro
espressivo
mf
D.C.

Air
(from Sonata No. 9)

Wolfgang Amadeus Mozart
(1756 - 1791)

Easy

Costel Puscoiu
(1951)

D.C.

March

Costel Puscoiu
(1951)

Allegro moderato

Greensleeves

Old English Song

Andante

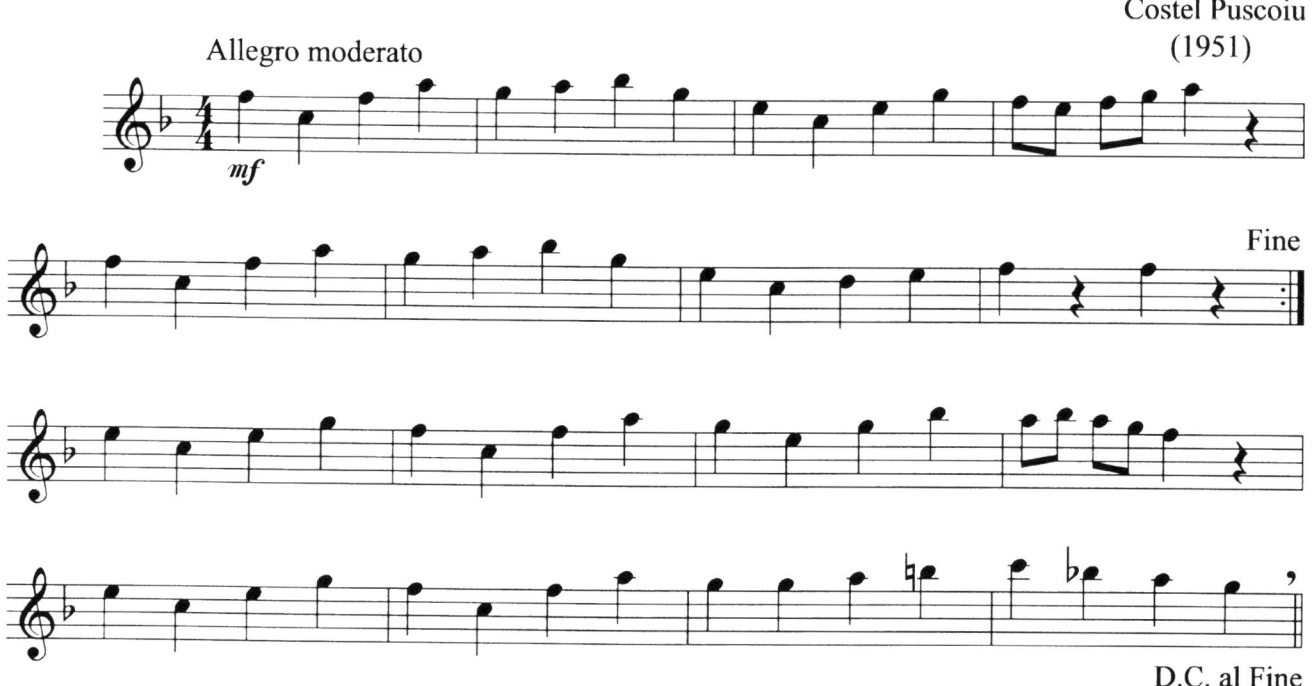

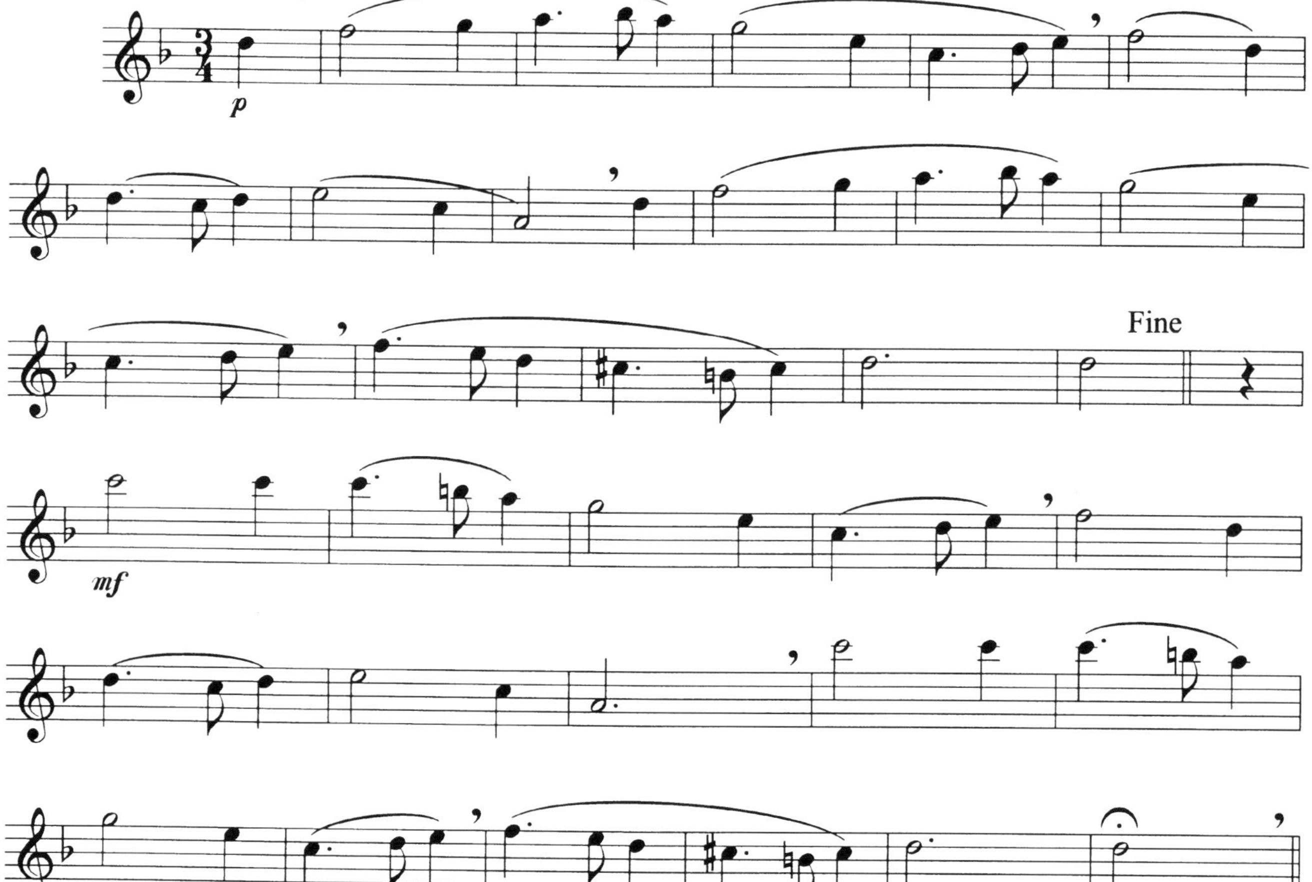

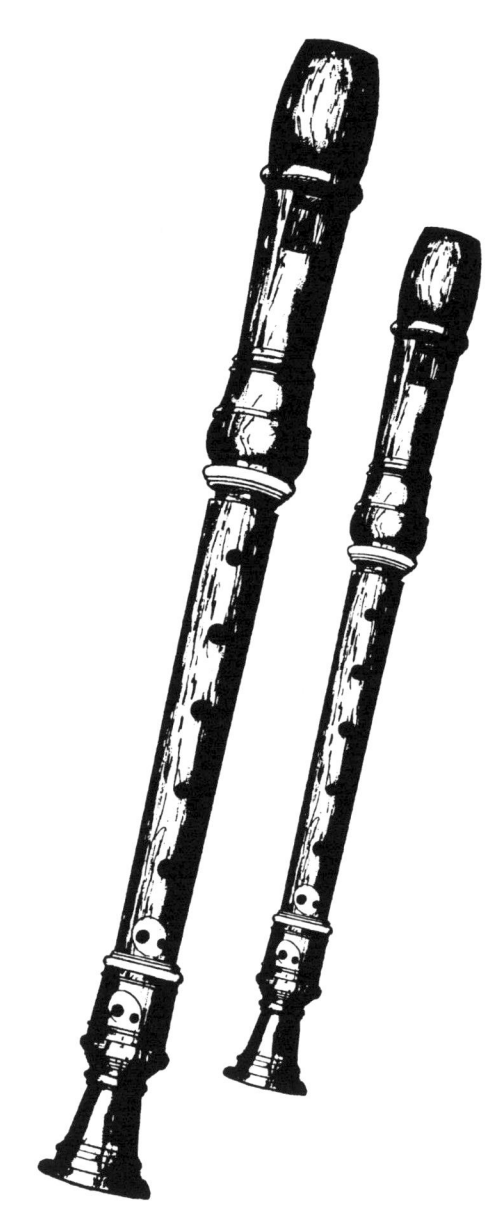

Moscow Nights

Children's Dance

Krakowiak

Pavane

Gabriel Fauré
(1845 - 1924)

Adagio
(from Clarinet Concerto)

Wolfgang Amadeus Mozart
(1756 - 1791)

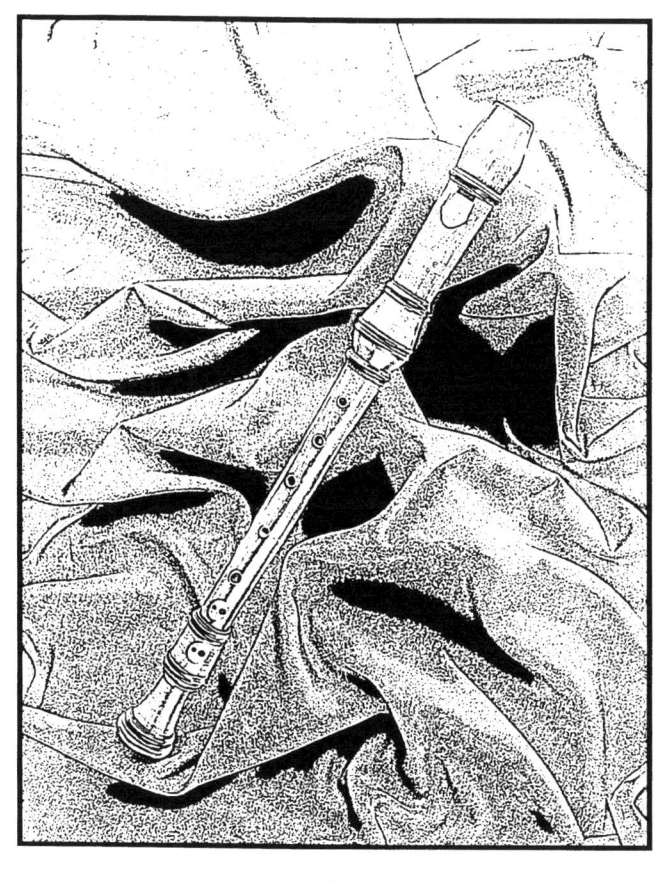

Album - leaf
(from "Lyric Pieces")

Edvard Grieg
(1843 - 1907)

Melody
(from "Scheherazade")

Nicolai Rimsky-Korsakov
(1844 - 1908)

Moscow Nights

Children's Dance

Costel Puscoiu
(1951)

Krakowiak

Polish Folk Song

Pavane

Gabriel Fauré
(1845 - 1924)

Adagio
(from Clarinet Concerto)

Wolfgang Amadeus Mozart
(1756 - 1791)

Prelude
(Op. 28, No. 7)

Frédéric Chopin
(1810 - 1849)

24

Two Pigeons

Argentinian Folk Song

Morning
(from "Peer Gynt")

Edvard Grieg
(1843 - 1907)

Allegretto pastorale

Album-leaf
(from "Lyric Pieces")

Edvard Grieg
(1843 - 1907)

29

Slavonic Dance
(Op. 46, No. 2)

Antonin Dvořák
(1841 - 1904)

Romance
(Op. 50)

Ludwig van Beethoven
(1770 - 1827)

31